EVERYBODY'S

ACTIVITY
BOOK

Pascale Estellon

EVERYBODY'S ACTIVITY

BOOK

CUT, STICK, COLOUR!

 Thames & Hudson

Shapes

Dots, lines and doodles

What goes

Reading and writing

Drawing and painting

Odds and

Shapes

Colour the circle **pink**.

Colour the square **blue**.

Colour the rectangles **green**.

Colour the triangle **red**.

Mr Pointy

Now colour all the shapes, using the same colours as before.

Using the stickers on sheet 1, fill up the three poles with paper lanterns,

so that the shapes get smaller and smaller towards the top.

Mrs Square

Mr Square

		o	o	o	o			
o	o	o	o	o	o	o	o	
		/	/	>	●			
		/	>	>	>	>		
		/	>	>	>			
		>	>	>	▪			
>		>	>	>	>			
▪			>					
*		▪	▪	▪				
▪	▪	▪	▪	▪	▪	▪	*	>
		*	*	*				
		▪	▪	▪				

To see Mr Square, colour in the squares using this colour code.

o   >   /   *   ▪

Use the stickers on sheet 2 to fill

in the white shapes.

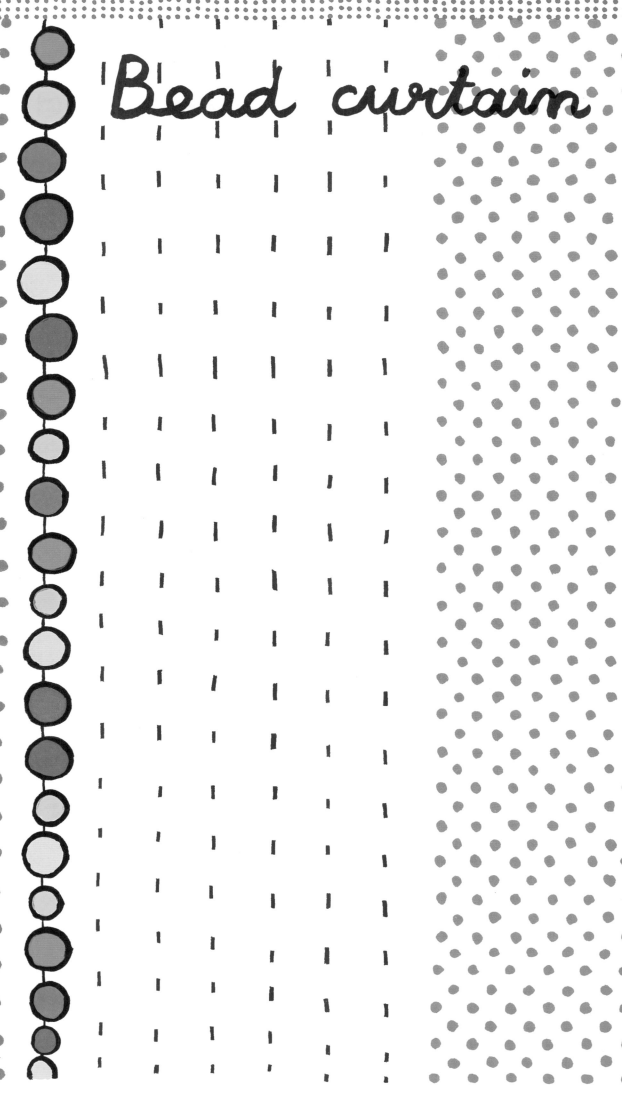

Bead curtain

Use your felt-tip pens to draw lots of coloured beads and make a curtain.

Cathy's curly hair

Use the stickers on sheet 1 to give Cathy lots of lovely curls.

Tablecloth

Give the flowers a coloured centre by using the stickers on sheet 3.

Carrots and peas

Use the pea and carrot stickers on sheet 3 to fill the plate for dinner.

Tropical islands

Help the fishermen to count the fish.

Then finish colouring in the picture.

Counting

1

On the head of Pat
is **one** pointy hat.

2

Surprise, surprise!
Two big
round eyes.

3

Oranges for tea!
Can you
draw **three**?

rhymes

4

Dogs have
four paws.
Mine does.
Does yours?

5

Do you like treats?
Here are
five sweets.

6

Six cherries red
In their basket bed.

Draw the missing shapes and finish the pictures.

Mak

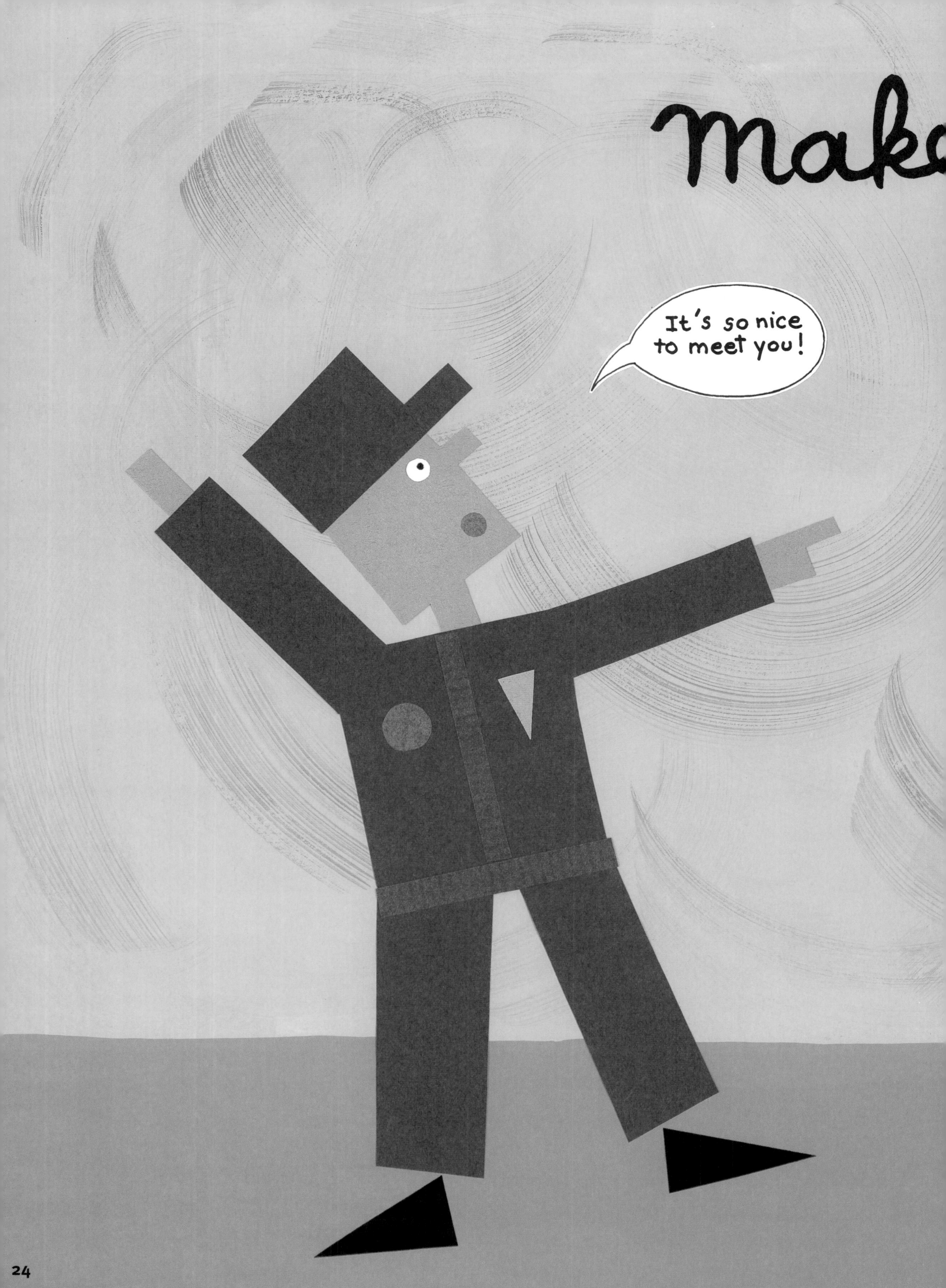

somebody new!

Hello there!

Use cut-out sheets 1 to 3 to cut out shapes and stick them down to make your own character.

1 2 3

4 5 6

7 8 9

10

Decorate the rest of the numbers up to 10.

Rhyme time

Ten oranges rolled down my street

I squashed them with my big flat feet

And though my feet now need a wash

I've made some lovely orange squash!

Decorate these three letters with patterns.

Dots, lines and doodles

How to draw dots, lines and doodles

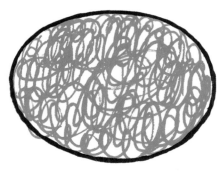

leaves

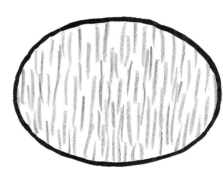

dry grass

green grass

tree bark

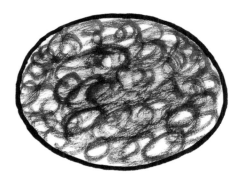

storm cloud

rain

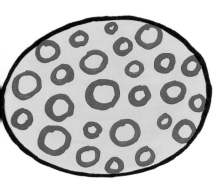 leopard skin

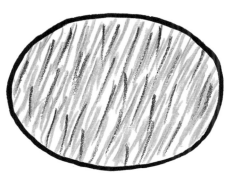 a lion's mane

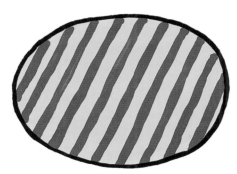 tiger skin

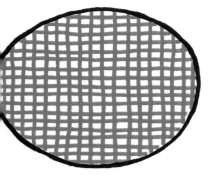 crocodile skin

 lion fur

 zebra skin

 fish scales

 panther or wolf fur

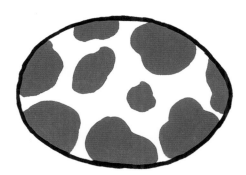 cow skin

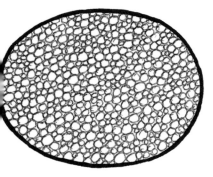 snake scales

 river water

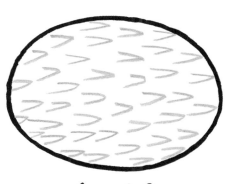 feathers

This little guide will help you to colour the following pages.

The **zebras** run through the **dry grass,** while the **crocodile** and the **flamingo** go fishing by the **river.** Who will catch the most **fish**?

Up in the **tree,** the **snake** looks down at the **lion,** the king of the beasts,

and wonders whether he has a crown hidden in his **mane**?

The **cows** are out in the field, nibbling the **green grass**. But the **storm clouds** in the sky mean that it's time to go home to their cowshed.

Look! Now it's pouring with **rain**! But don't worry, the cows are warm and safe inside.

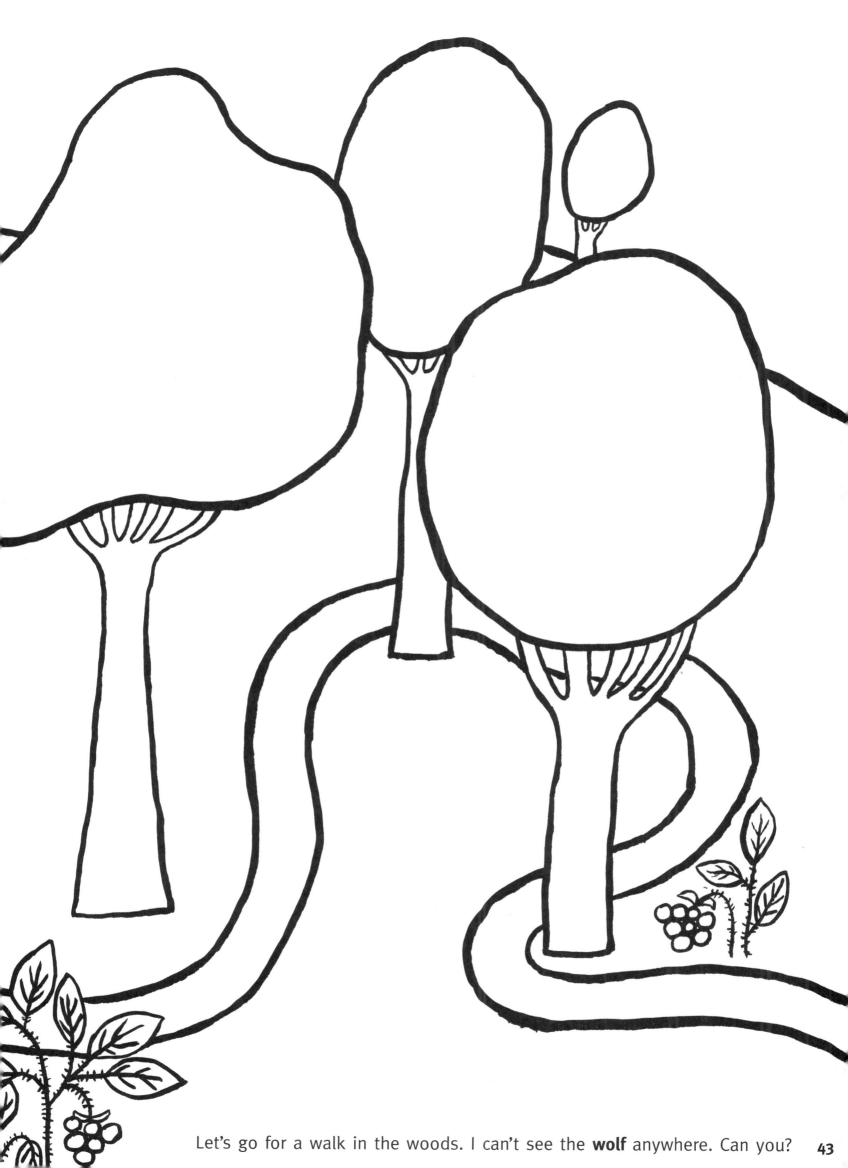

Let's go for a walk in the woods. I can't see the **wolf** anywhere. Can you?

What would this elephant look like if he had a trunk made of **crocodile skin**, legs

like a **leopard, snake scales** on his ears and a body with **zebra stripes**?

Finish colouring the fur of these big cats.

THE TIGER

THE BLACK PANTHER

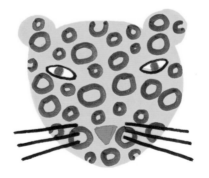

AND THE LEOPARD

Colour the letters so that they match each animal's fur!

Rhyme time

The tiger has stripes on his back

The panther's coat is sleek and black

The leopard has a hundred spots

Count them, there are lots and lots!

Decorate this rhyme with some drawings of your own.

Decorate these three letters.

What goes where?

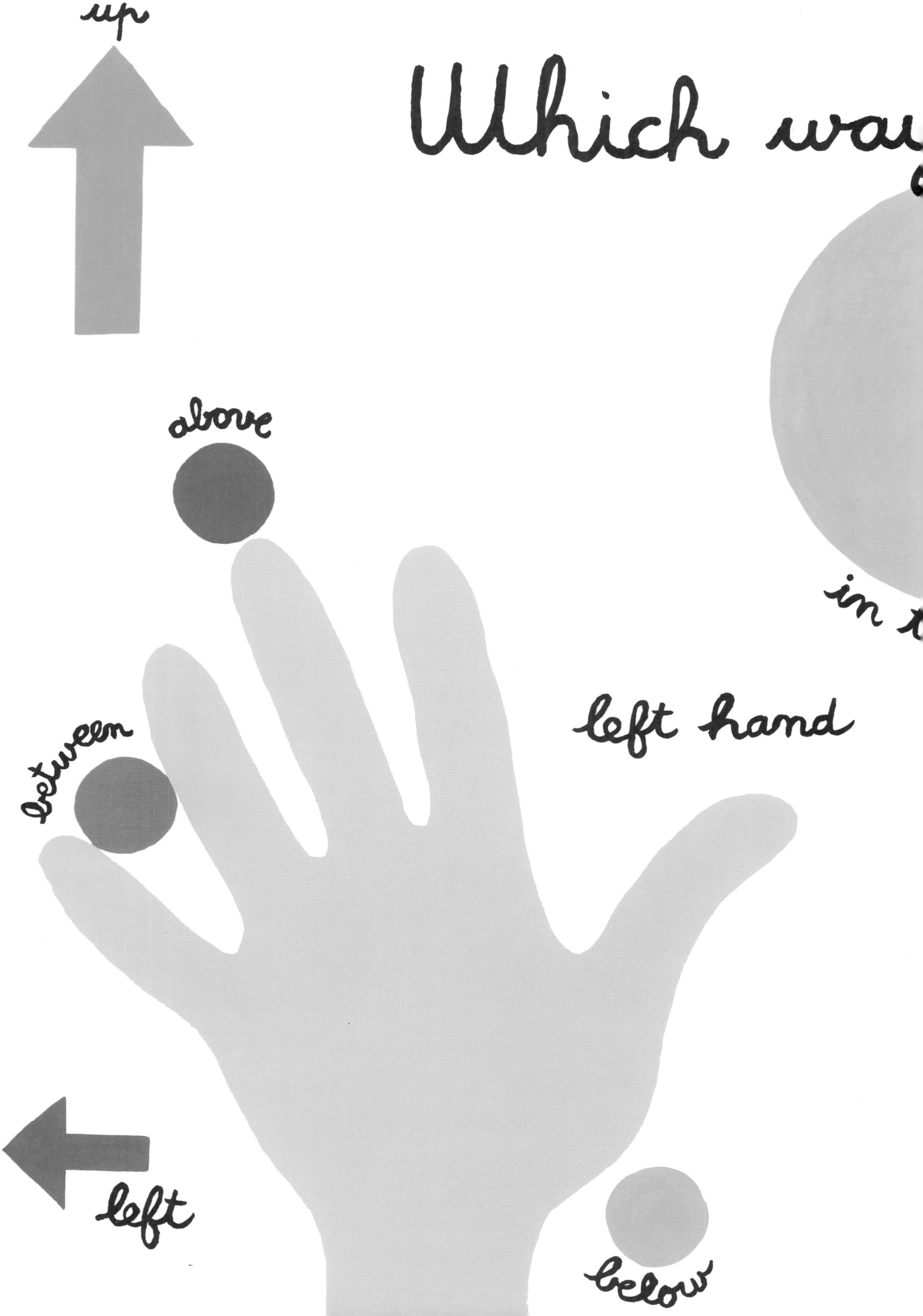
Which wa
up
above
between
left hand
in t
left
below

s which ?

middle

right

right hand

beside

down

The bus driver sits right at the front. Behind him, an old lady with glasses is looking out of the window. Behind the old lady, there's a man in a green hat with a newspaper. At the back of the bus is a boy reading a comic. In front of the boy, there's a mother with her baby.

Behind the man in the green hat, a girl is eating a strawberry ice cream. When the lady in the flowery dress finds her seat, the bus will be ready to go! Use the stickers on sheet 4 to put all the passengers in the right place.

Lots of people are standing in the queue at the cinema. Use sticker sheet 4 and make sure that everyone's in the right place. There are three people standing between the man in blue jeans and the woman in red trousers. In front of the woman in red trousers, there's one person. In front of that person, there's a woman chatting to her friend.

At the cinema

Behind the woman at the front of the queue, there's one person. It's the last show of the day and there are only eight seats left. Will there be enough room for everyone who wants to see the film?

We're moving house today!

Here's the kitchen

Here's the living room

You'll need sticker sheet 5 and cut-out sheet 4.

Here's the playroom

You'll need sticker sheet 6 and cut-out sheet 5.

Here's the garden

You'll need sticker sheet 6 and cut-out sheet 5.

Find the missing pieces of the broken vase and plate (cut-out sheet 6).

fix it ?

Then cut them out and stick them in the right places.

Decorate these five letters.

Reading and writing

Read the words and colour in the man.

Word pictures

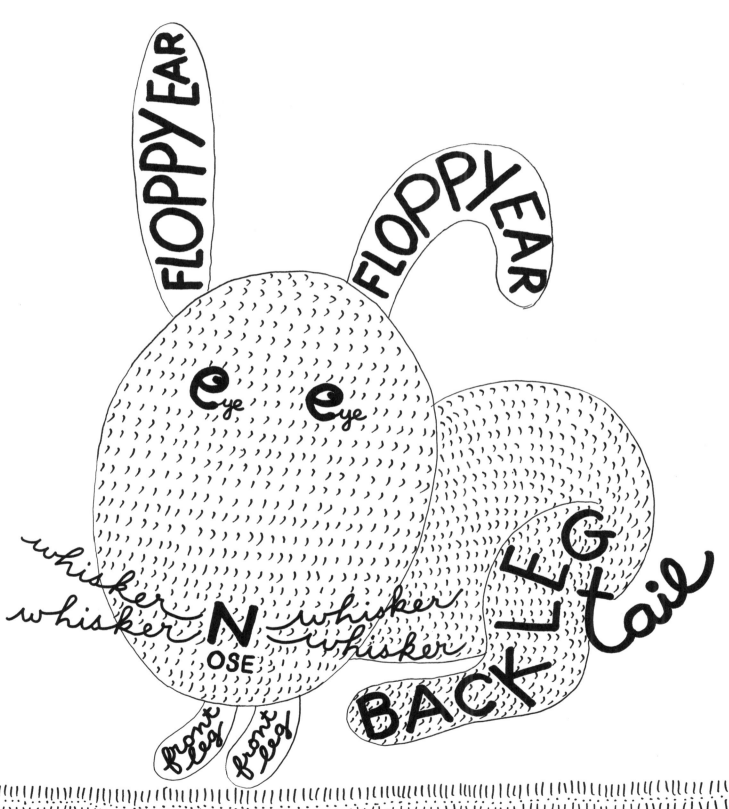

Read the words and colour in the rabbit.

Who are these characters?
Work out their names and fill in the speech bubbles. Then colour them in!

Word pictures

sunshine
sunshine
sunshine
sunshine

THE

FOREST

Picture words

Finish drawing these picture words and fill in the spaces.

rain · rain · rain · rain · rain

String

KNITTING

FIRE

shadow

Turn these words into pictures by adding your own drawings.

snow

FiReWORKS

party

cow

BRiCKS

My picture book

girl

dog

boy

birds

winter colours

house

cat

castle

sky

Look for the pictures that match these words on cut-out

tree

guitar

leaves

daisy

spring colours

tulips

dancer

vase

butterfly

sheets 7 and 8. Then cut them out and stick them on.

Birds

Ducklings learn
to swim and play
Spring will soon
be on its way

Up above
the seagulls cry
Soaring through
the summer sky

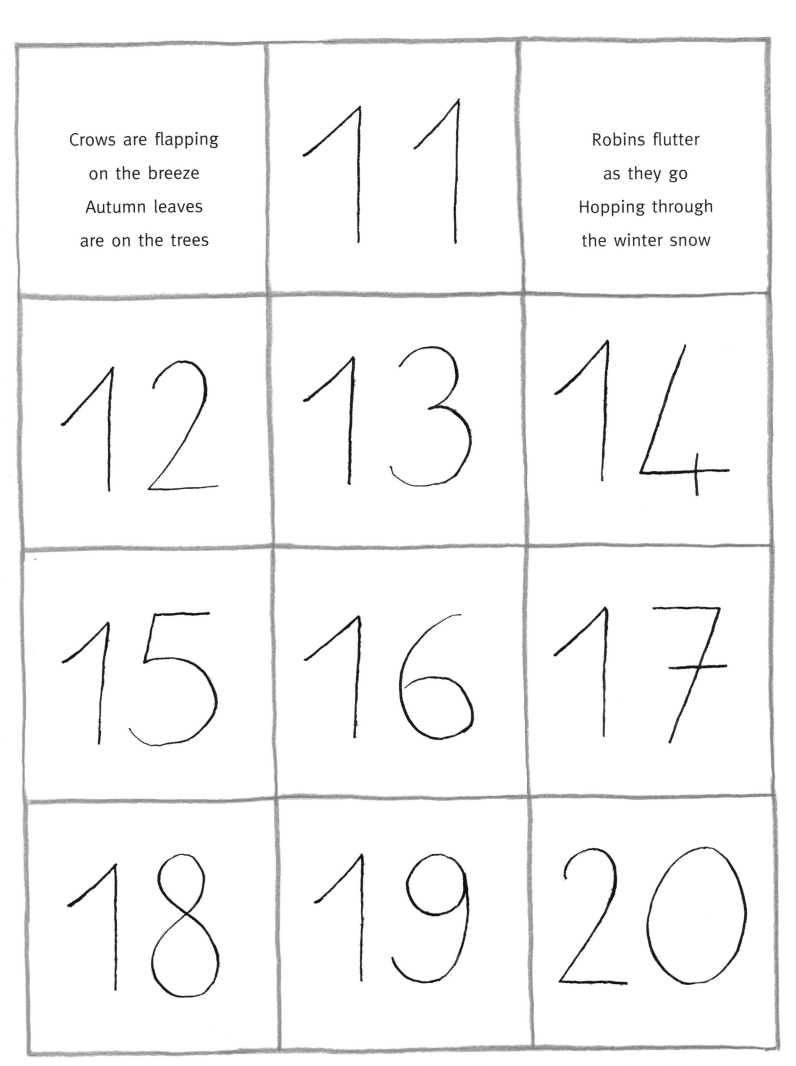

Crows are flapping
on the breeze
Autumn leaves
are on the trees

11

Robins flutter
as they go
Hopping through
the winter snow

12   13   14

15   16   17

18   19   20

Turn the rest of the numbers into birds, and learn to count to twenty!

Decorate these five letters.

Drawing and painting

coloured pencils

I can draw

felt-tip pens

crayons

spatter-painting with an old toothbrush →

ballpoint pen

watercolour paints

and paint with...

a ballpoint pen with
four different colours

fingerpainting

poster paints

cotton buds
dipped
in paint

potato printing
(or use a carrot)

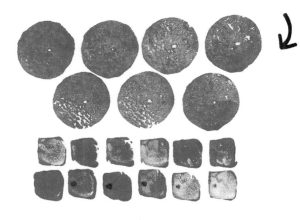

cut-out
paper

These two horses look the same as each other, but colour the

draw a new background and border to make them look totally different.

Paint these portraits any way you like

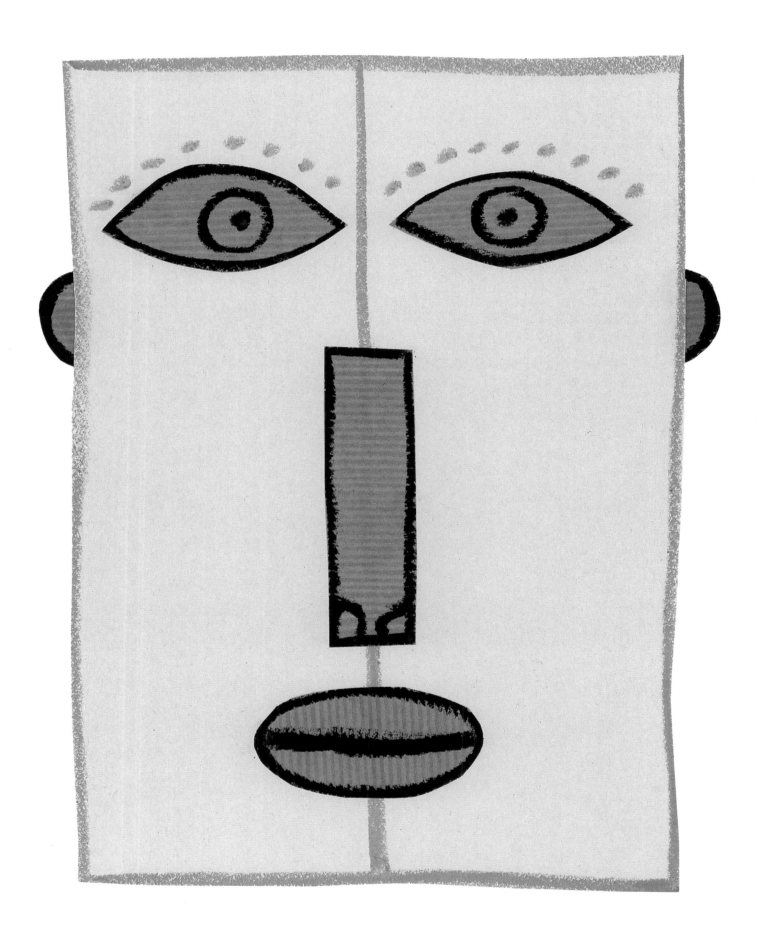

Decorate these masks with potato printing.

Draw an apple, using the photo to help you.

Draw a cat, using the photo to help you.

Draw some tomatoes and courgettes, using the photo to help you.

Draw a vase of flowers, using the photo to help you.

Draw the missing half of these faces.

Decorate these three letters

Odds and ends

Spring is here! Draw leaves on the tree.

Who's on the path? Draw them.

There are ducks on the water. Draw them.

There are cows in the field. Draw them.

This girl is taking her dog for a walk. Draw the dog and fill in the background.

Mrs Veg

Here's Mrs Veg.

Mr Veg

Finish Mr Veg, using cut-out sheets 9 and 10.

Violet

Finish Violet Veg, using cut-out sheets 9 and 10.

Victor

Here's Victor Veg.

Vicky and Vincent

Finish Vincent, using cut-out sheets 9 and 10.

Decorate this letter.

Translated from the French *Mon premier livre d'activités*, first published by Éditions du Panama.

First published in the United Kingdom in 2007 by
Thames & Hudson Ltd, 181A High Holborn, London WC1V 7QX

www.thamesandhudson.com

Original edition © 2006 Éditions du Panama, Paris
This edition © 2007 Thames & Hudson Ltd, London

Reprinted 2008

British Library Cataloguing-in-Publication Data
A catalogue record for this book is available from the British Library

ISBN 978-0-500-28691-3

Printed in Thailand